AF483286

TO MY SISTER,

WHO SOMEHOW MANAGED TO LOCKHERSELF IN THE BATHROOM,

ON DAYS WHEN YOU DON'T FEEL YOUR BEST

## FOREWARD

UNIVERSITY BRINGS WITH IT A TRANSFORMATIVE JOURNEY, A JOURNEY FILLED WITH EXCITEMENT, CHALLENGES, AND GROWTH. I REMEMBER VIVIDLY THE MIXED EMOTIONS I FELT WHEN STARTING THIS NEW CHAPTER. THE THRILL OF NEWFOUND INDEPENDENCE AND ANXIETY FROM THE UNFAMILIARITY. IN A HOPE OF TRULEY DISCOVERING WHO I WANTED MYSELF TO BECOME. THESE WORDS AND CERTAIN QUOTES RESONATED WITH ME AND OFTEN BECAME MYANCHOR.

THIS BOOK COMPILES THOSE QUOTES. IT'S MY GIFT TO YOU, DEAR READER, AND ESPECIALLY TO MY YOUNGER SISTER. ONE WHO IS HERSELF AT THE BRINK OF STARTING THE SAME CHAPTER I DID THREE YEARS AGO. WE'VE SHARED COUNTLESS MOMENTS GROWING UP. NOW, AS WE EMBARK ON OUR SEPARATE PATHS, REMEMBER MY SUPPORT REMAINS UNWAVERING, EVEN IF WE ARE MILES APART.

TO MY SISTER, THIS BOOK IS A TESTAMENT TO OUR BOND. EACH QUOTE, A REMINDER THAT I'M WITH YOU IN SPIRIT. I HOPETHESE WORDS OFFER YOU THE SAME ENCOURAGEMENT AND WISDOM THEY DID TO ME.

TO THE READERS, MAY THIS COLLECTION OF AFFIRMATIONS BE YOUR COLLEGE COMPANION. LET THESE QUOTES REMIND YOU

THAT YOU ARE NEVER TRULY ALONE. THERE IS ALWAYS SOMEONE WHO UNDERSTANDS. SOMEONE WHO HAS WALKED A SIMILAR PATH AND WHO BELIEVES IN YOUR ABILITY TO OVERCOME ANY OBSTACLE.

USE THIS BOOK AS A SOURCE OF INSPIRATION AND GUIDANCE, ONE THAT HELPS YOU FIND CONFIDENCE IN UNCERTAINITIES. UNIVERSIY IS ABOUT PERSONAL GROWTH, NOT JUST ACADEMICS. EMBRACE EXPERIENCES. LEARN FROM CHALLENGES AND SHAPE YOUR DESTINY.

WITH HEARTFELT WISHES FOR YOUR SUCCESS AND HAPPINESS.

ARISIA

DREAM IT, BELIEVE IT, ACHIEVE IT.

THERE IS A PAST VERSION OF YOU WHO IS PROUDOF HOW FAR YOU HAVE COME.

WHEN YOU CHOOSE LOVE,
I HOPE YOU CHOOSE YOUSELF TOO

LESS PERFECTION, MORE AUTHENTICITY

RISKING IS BETTER THAN REGRETTING.

BREATHE DARLING....

BE A BAD BITCH AND A GOOD PERSON,

IT'S OKAY TO BE BOTH.

DON'T BE AFARID OF LOSING PEOPLE.
BE AFRAID OF LOSING YOURSELF TRYING TO PLEASEEVERYONE AROUND YOU.

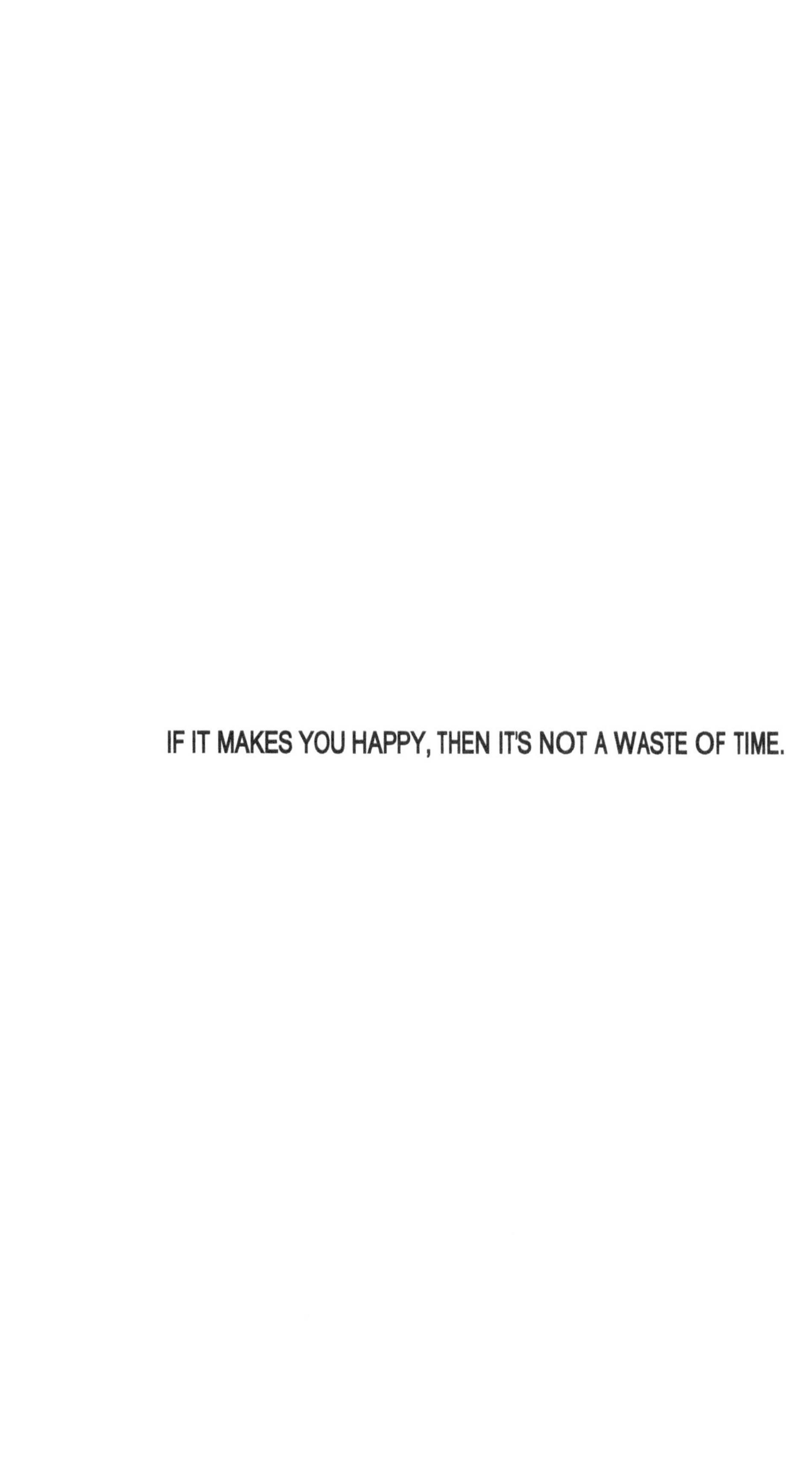
IF IT MAKES YOU HAPPY, THEN IT'S NOT A WASTE OF TIME.

LEARN TO BE DONE WITH PEOPLE,NOT MAD, NOT BOTHERED JUST DONE.

DON'T REGRET BEING GOOD TO PEOPLE.

CALL PEOPLE WHO FEEL LIKE HOME,

WHEN EVERYTHING ELSE IN YOUR LIFE SEEMS TO BE FALLING APART

GO WORKOUT.

SOMETIMES YOU WIN, SOMETIMES YOU LEARN

YOUR ONLY LIMIT IS WHAT YOU BIND YOURSELF TO.

IT'S YOUR STORY,
HIT THEM WITH A PLOT TWIST.

IT'S A BAD DAY, NOT A BAD LIFE!

TRY... AND THAT'S ENOUGH.

YOU HAVE BEEN ASSIGNED THIS MOUNTAIN TOSHOW
OTHERS IT CAN BE MOVED

CHAOTIC DUMBASS ENERGY

TIME HEALS.

ENJOY THE NOW!

EXIST IN MOMENTS

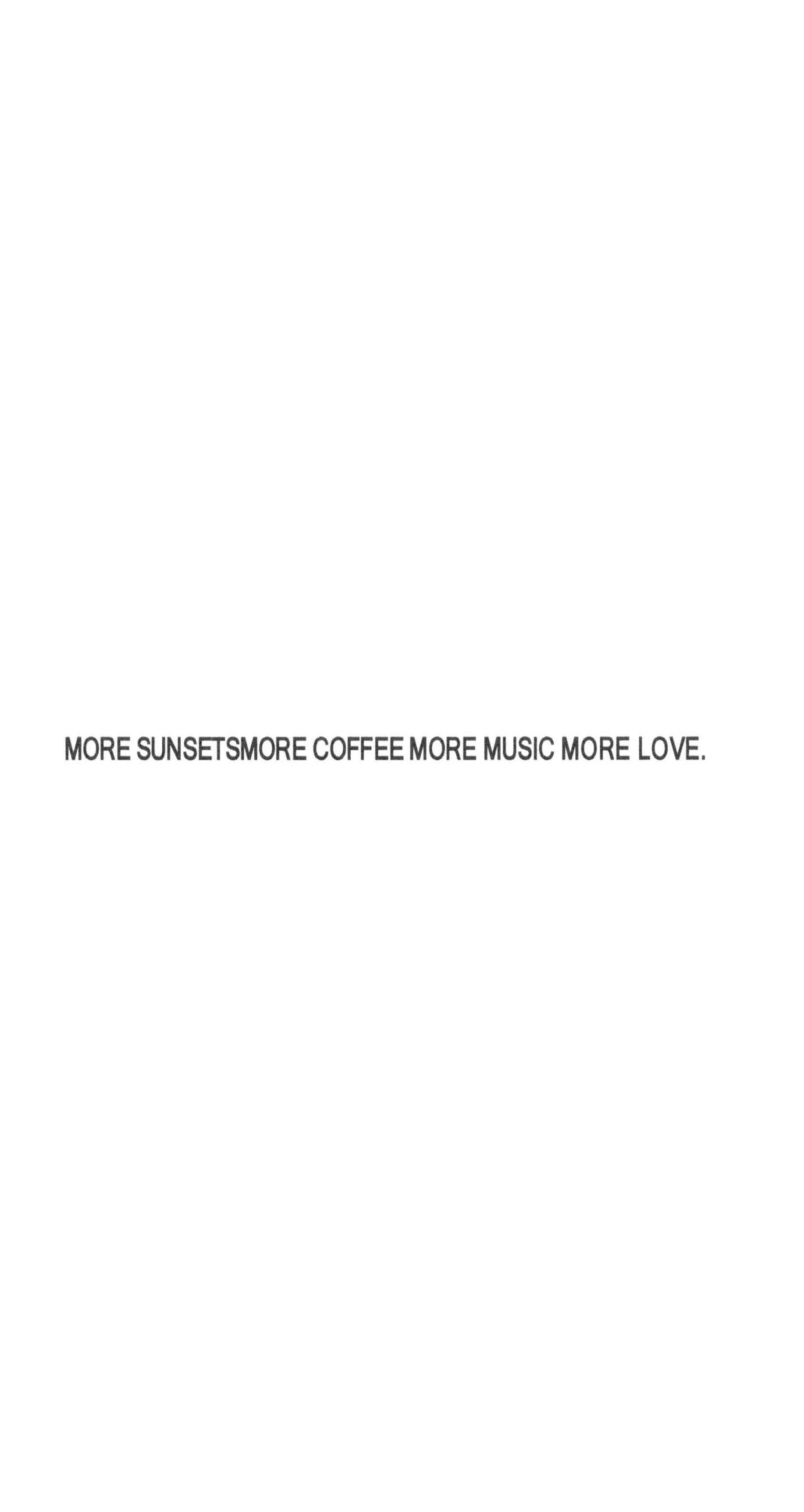
MORE SUNSETSMORE COFFEE MORE MUSIC MORE LOVE.

GIVE A DAMN, OCCASIONALLY.

SLOW PROGRESS IS BETTER THAN NO PROGRESS

LIVE . LAUGH . LOVE .

THE RIGHT PEOPLE STAY.

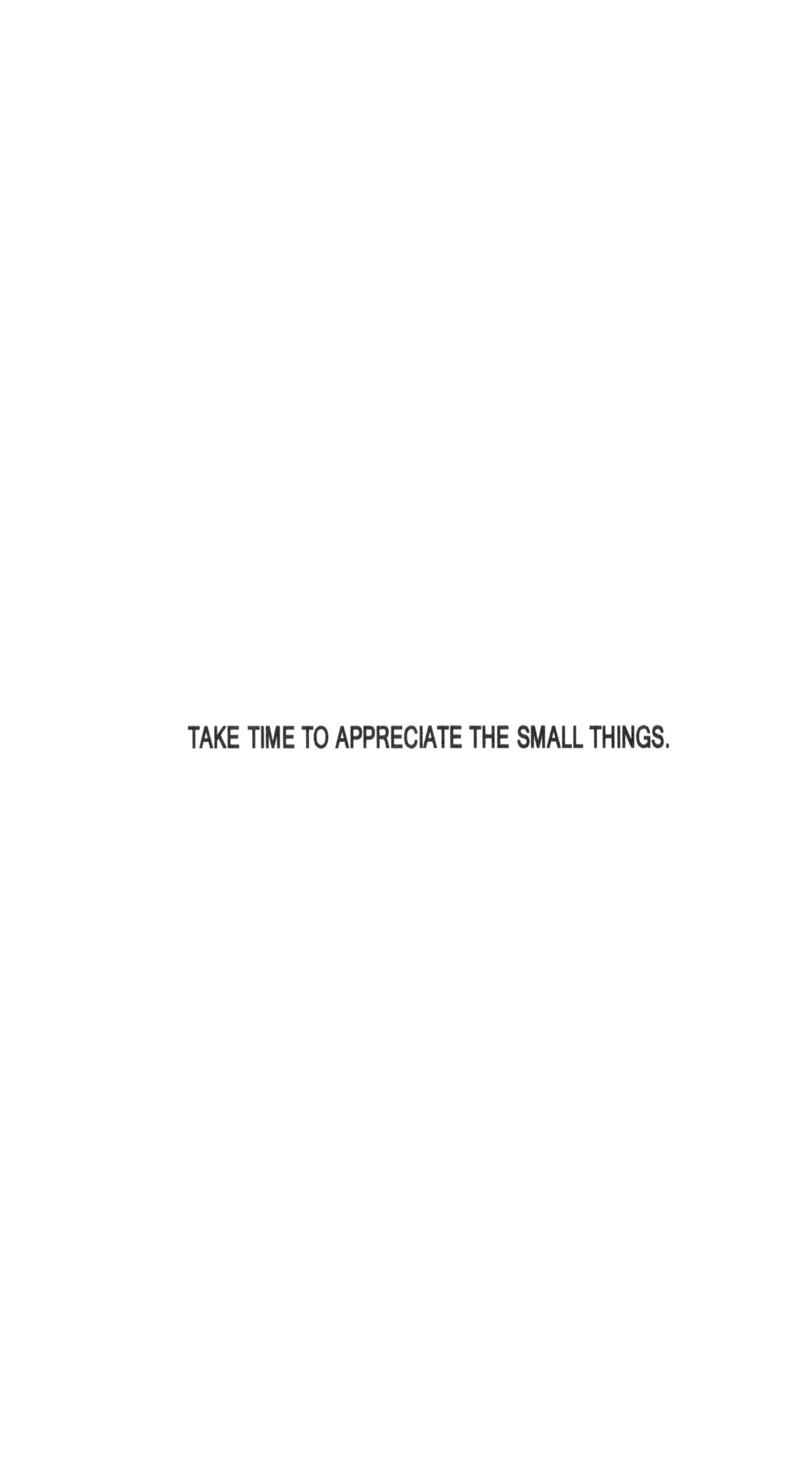

TAKE TIME TO APPRECIATE THE SMALL THINGS.

THINGS ONLY HAVE POWER OVER YOU IFYOU ALLOW THEM TO.

LET YOUR FAITH BE BIGGER THAN YOUR FEARS.

IF NOT US, WHO? IF NOT NOW, WHEN?

OLD WAYS DON'T OPEN NEW DOORS

WHAT IF I FALL?
OH DARLING, BUT WHAT IF YOU FLY?

WE ALL WEAR SCARS -
FIND SOMEONE WHO MAKES YOURS FEEL BEAUTIFUL

DO SOMETHING TODAY
THAT YOUR FUTURE SELF WILL THANK YOU FOR

SOLITUDE OVER TOXICITY

IT'S OKAY TO START OVER. IT'S OKAY TO ASK FOR HELP.
IT'S OKAY TO SAY NO.
IT'S OKAY TO NOT BE OKAY.

IN SILENCE YOU WILL FIND YOUR ANSWERS

LEARNING AND GROWING DOES NOT HAPPEN WHEN ITS EASY.

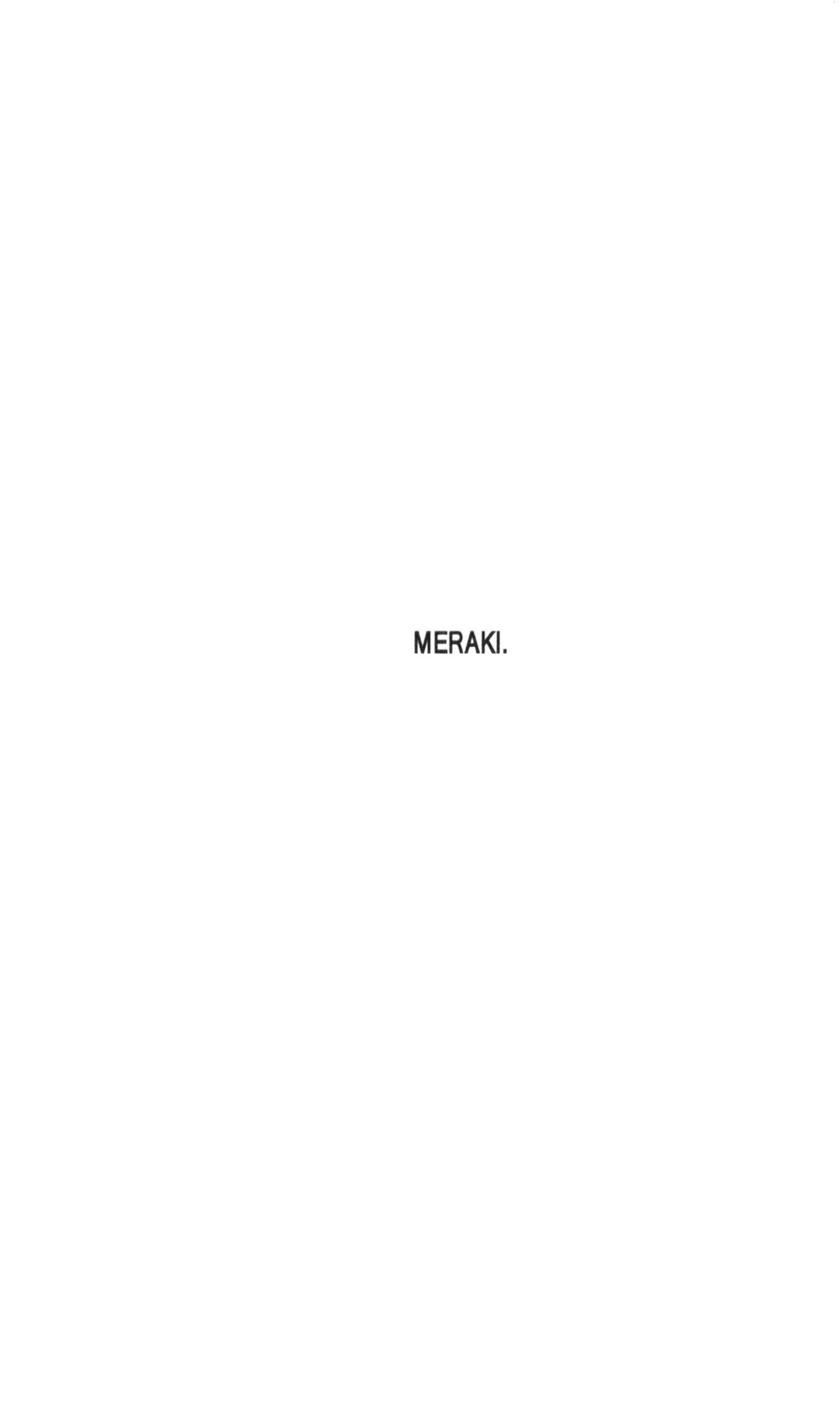
MERAKI.

ONE DAY THE PAIN WILL MAKE SENSE TO YOU.

KEEP GOING, DARLINGYOU GOT THIS.

CONSISTENCY IS MORE IMPORTANT THAN PERFECTION

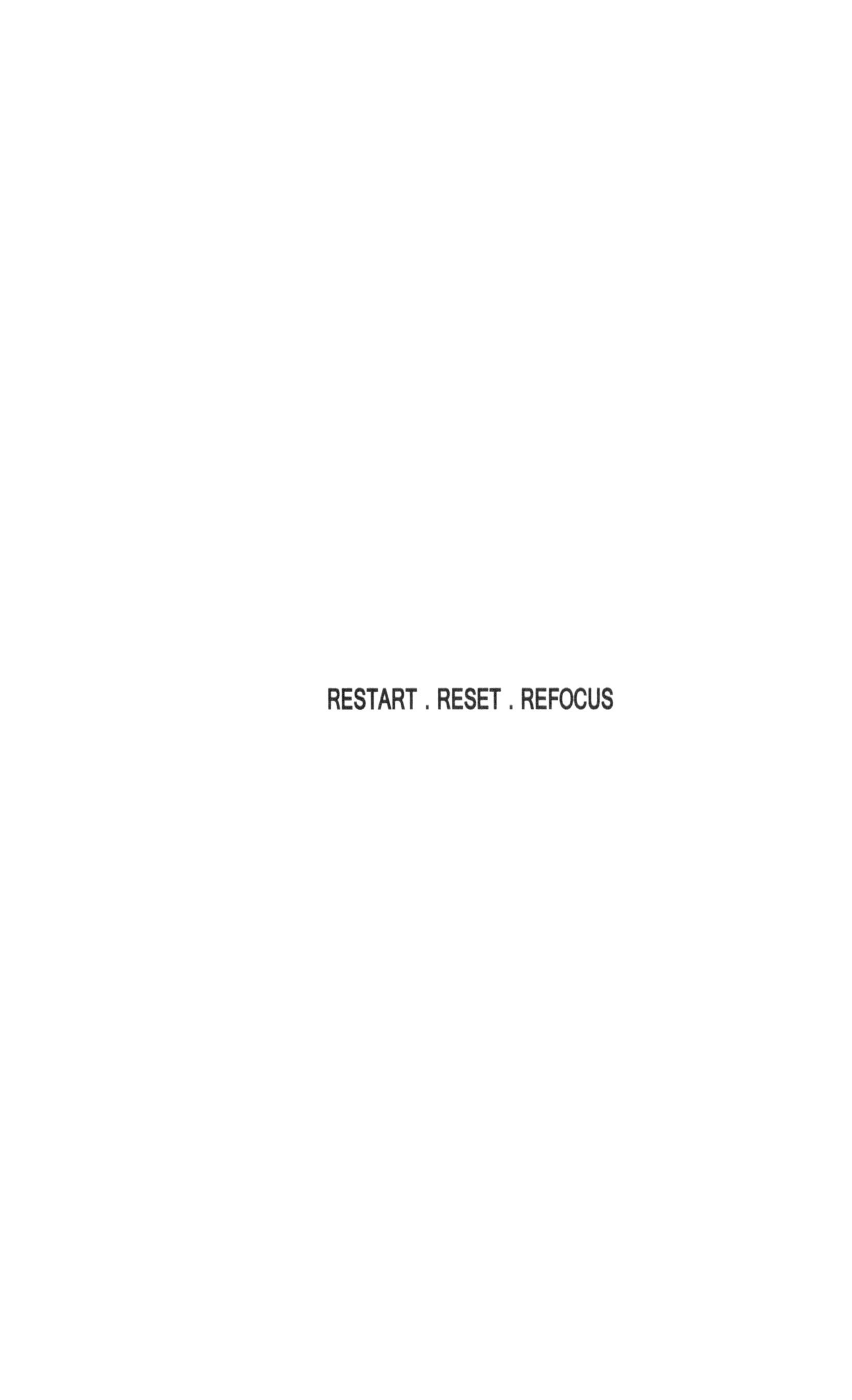

RESTART . RESET . REFOCUS

DON'T ADAPT THE ENERGY IN THE ROOM, INFLUENCE THE ENERGY IN THE ROOM.

SELF DOUBT KILLS MORE DREAMS ,THAN FAILURE EVER COULD

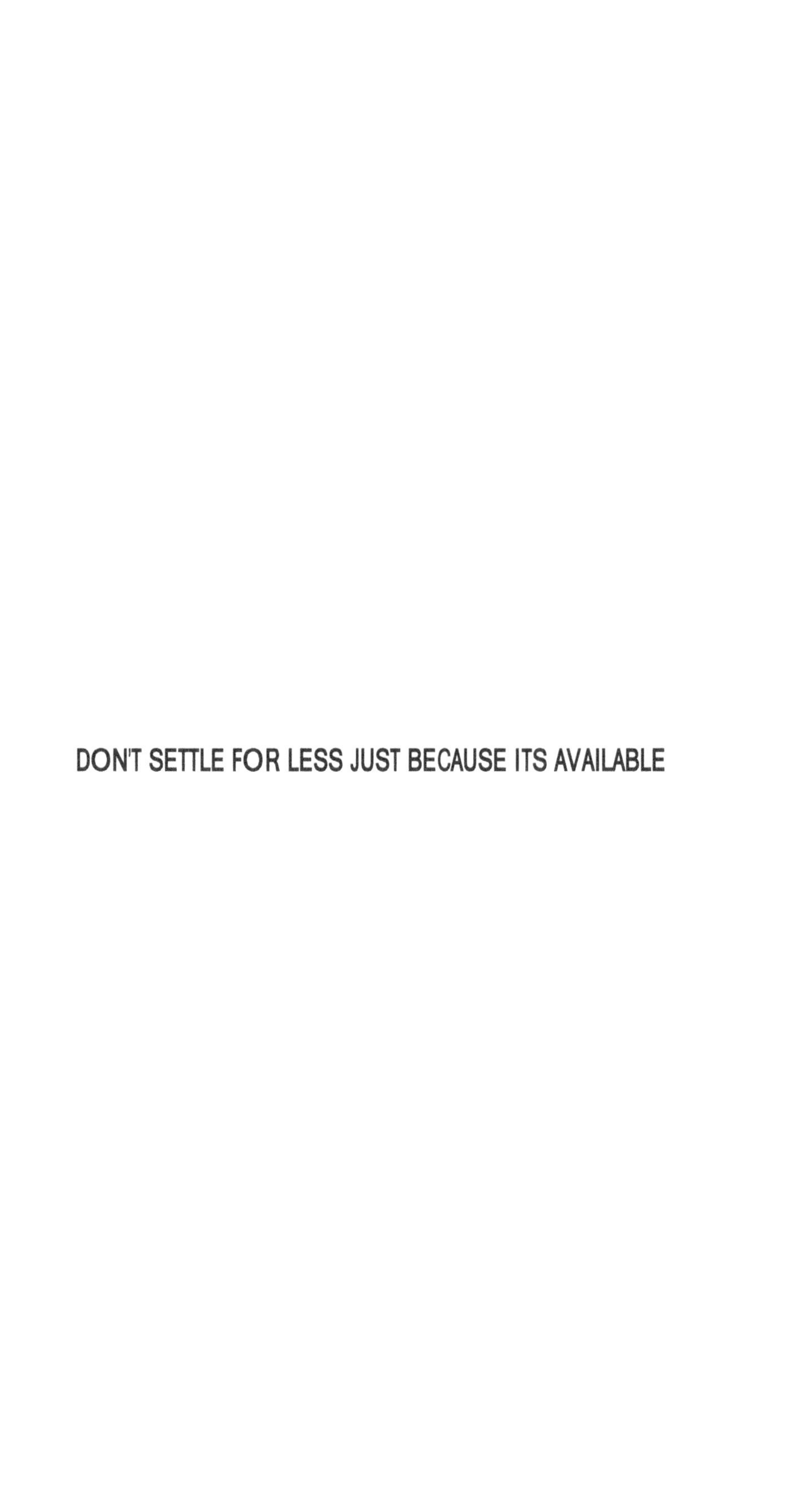

DON'T SETTLE FOR LESS JUST BECAUSE ITS AVAILABLE

LEARN TO BE OKAY WITH PEOPLE NOT KNOWINGYOUR
SIDE OF THE STORY.
YOU HAVE NOTHING TO PROVE TO ANYONE

YOU VS.YOU.

GREAT THINGS TAKE TIME.

SAY YES TO NEW ADVENTURES!

REMEMBER WHY YOU STARTED

PATIENCE.

OBSESSION BEATS TALENT.

~~WHY IS THIS HAPPENING TO ME?~~

WHAT IS THIS TEACHING ME?

MAKE THIS COMEBACK PERSONAL.

SOMETIMES MAKE THE DECISION THAT WILL BREAKYOUR HEART BUT WILL GIVE PEACE TO YOUR SOUL.

YOUR LIFE WILL NEVER BE YOURS IF YOU CARE WHAT OTHER PEOPLE THINK.

PROTECT YOUR PEACE

YOU ARE ENOUGH. YOU HAVE A VOICE.YOU ARE SEEN. YOU ARE CAPABLE.

BE SOMEBODY WHO MAKES EVERYBODY FEEL LIKE SOMEBODY.

SOMETIMES THINGS HAVE TO GO VERYWRONG BEFORE THEY CAN BE RIGHT

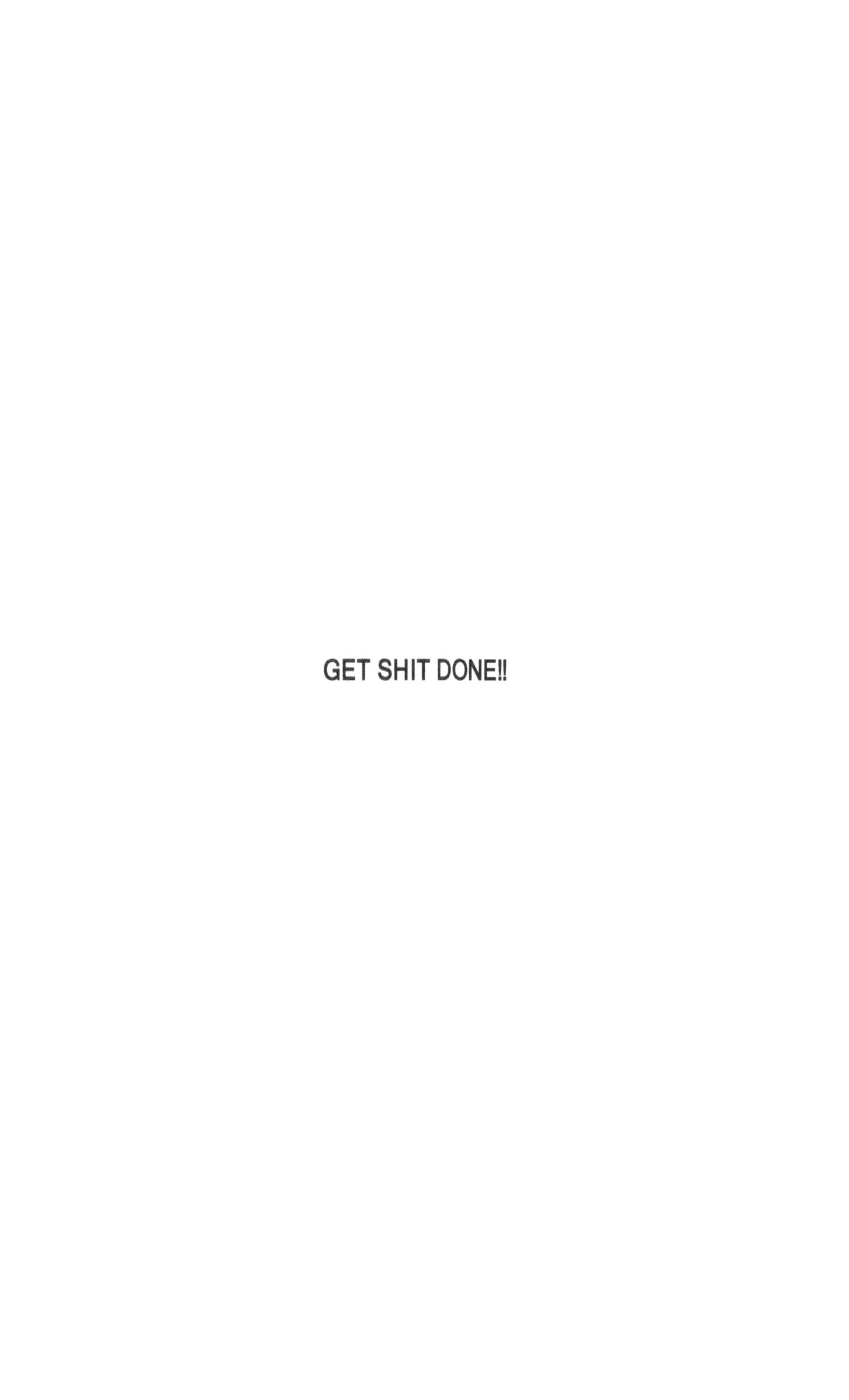
GET SHIT DONE!!

YOU JUST HAVE TO TAKE IT ONE"ARE YOU FUCKING KIDDING ME" AT A TIME.

CREATE A LIFE YOU CAN'T WAIT TO WAKE UP TO.

WHEN LIFE PUTS YOU IN DIFFICULT SITUATIONS SAY'TRY ME'

WE BLAME SOCIETY BUT WE ARE SOCIETY.

DON'T EVER LET THE SAME PEOPLE DISSAPOINT YOU TWICE

YOU CAN MUTE PEOPLE IN REAL LIFE TOO ITS CALLED 'BOUNDARIES'

YOU'LL GET JUDGED EITHER WAY,
SO MAY AS WELL PICK THE FUN OPTION.

# FRIENDSHIPS AND RELATIONSHIPSARE A TWO-WAY STREET

FIND YOUR TRIBE.LOVE THEM HARD.

YOU WERE OKAY BEFORE YOU WILL BE OKAY AFTER.

UNPLANNED MOMENTS ARE ALWAYS BETTER THAN PLANNED ONES.

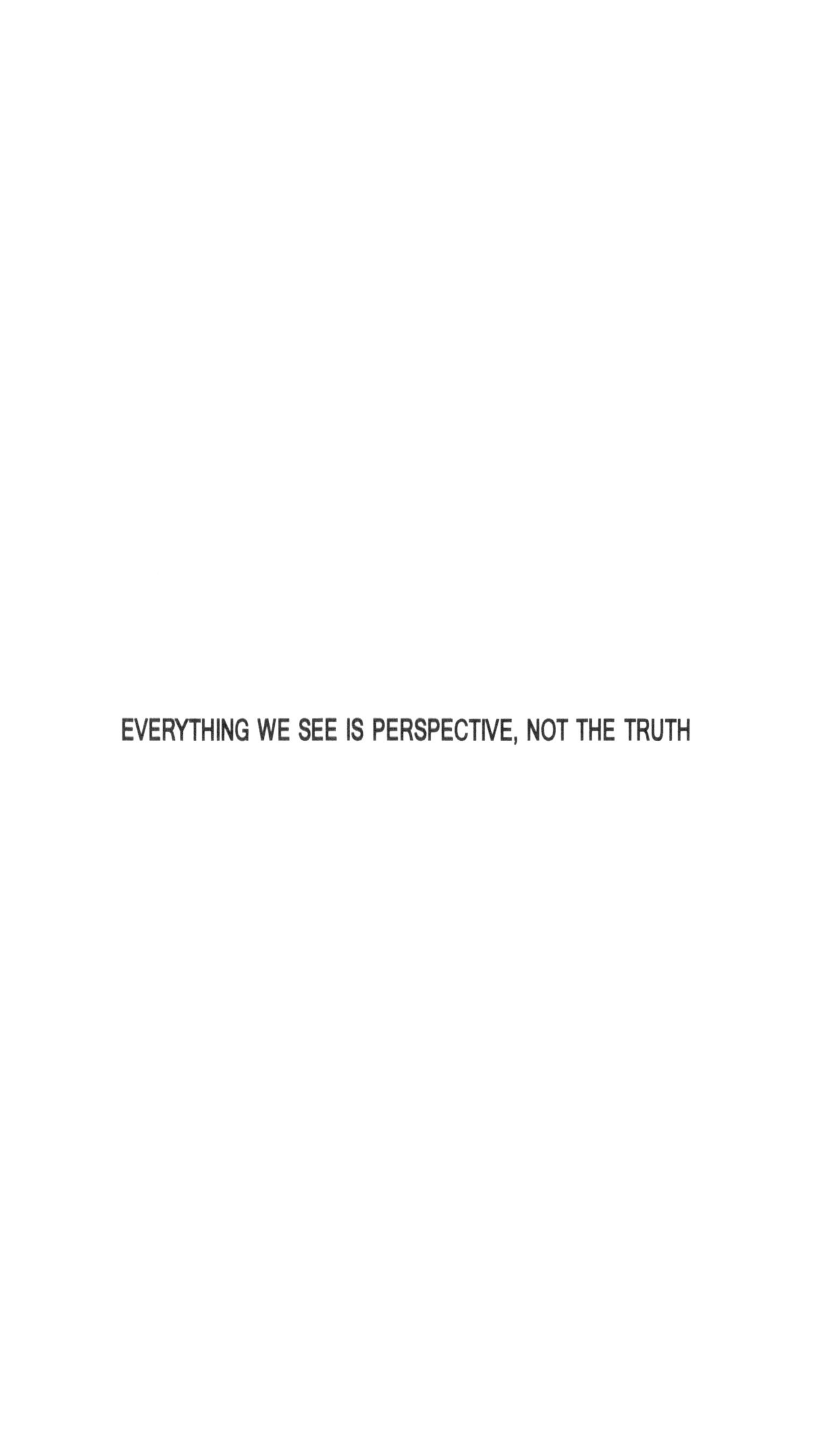
EVERYTHING WE SEE IS PERSPECTIVE, NOT THE TRUTH

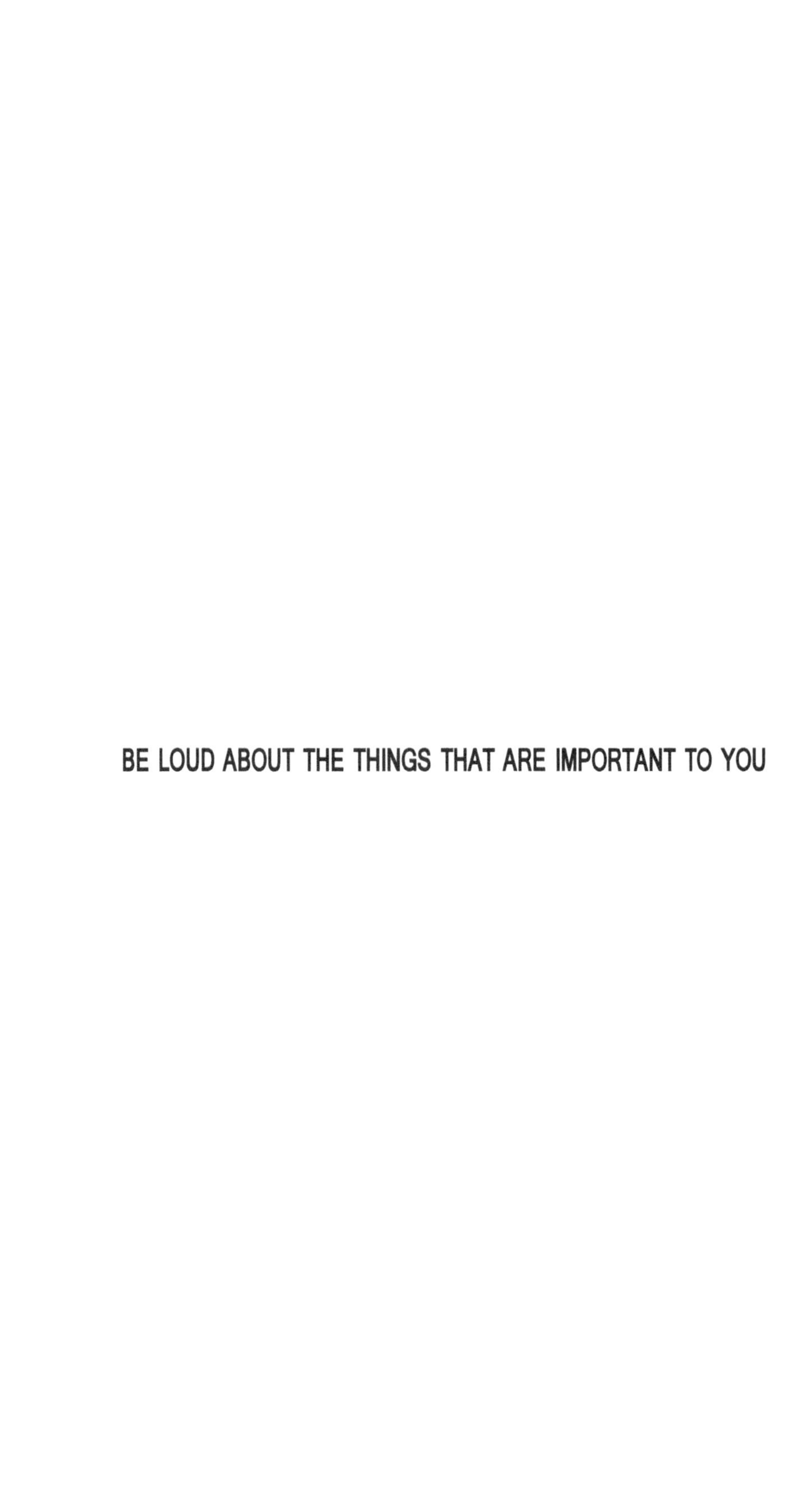
BE LOUD ABOUT THE THINGS THAT ARE IMPORTANT TO YOU

NO ONE IS YOU AND THAT'S YOUR POWER

DISCIPLINE LEADS TO HABITS, HABITS LEAD TO CONSISTENCY, CONSISTENCY LEADS TO GROWTH

LIVE LESS OUT OF HABIT, ANDMORE OUT OF INTENT

ACT WITHOUT
EXPECTATIONS.

"AUT VIAM INVANIAM AUT FACIAM"

BUILT, NOT BOUGHT. EARNED, NOT GIVEN. HUSTLED, NOT HANDED.

TO BE REAL IS TO BE RARE.

KAIZEN.

YOU ARE ALLOWED TO MAKE A BIG DEALABOUT THINGS
THAT ARE IMPORTANT YOU

BEING QUIET DOES NOT EQUATE TOBEING BLIND.

HOLD THE VISION.

SHE WAS NEVER QUIET READYBUT SHE WAS BRAVE.
THE UNIVERSE LISTENS TO THE BRAVE.

READ THAT BOOK ON YOUR TO READING LIST

FATA VIAM INVENIENT

THINK ABOUT WHAT YOU WANT, TALK ABOUT WHATYOU WANT, IT'S ALL YOU HAVE TO DO TO ATTRACT WHAT YOU WANT.

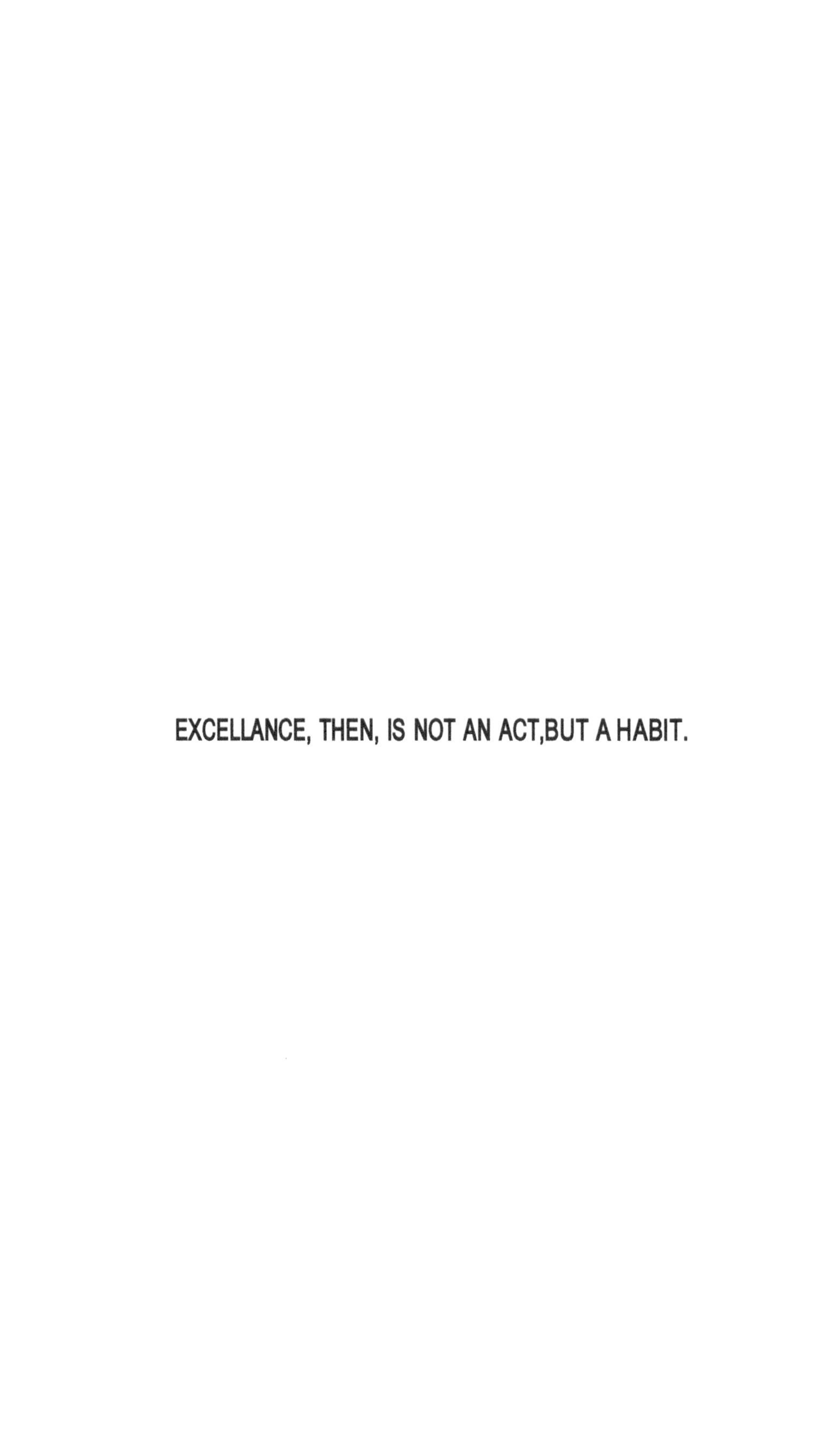

EXCELLANCE, THEN, IS NOT AN ACT,BUT A HABIT.

A MISTAKE IS SUCCES IN PROGRESS.

IF YOU KNOW WHENCE YOU CAME, THERE ISREALLY NO LIMIT TO WHERE YOU CAN GO.

THE ONLY WAY OUT IS THROUGH.

YOU CAN'T ALWAYS DO GREAT THINGS, BUT YOU CAN DO SMALL THINGS WITH GREAT LOVE

THE WORLD IS MORE MALLEABLE THAN YOU THINK,
ANDIT'S WAITING FOR YOU TO HAMMER IT INTO SHAPE.

START WHERE YOU ARE.USE WHAT YOU HAVE. DO WHAT YOU CAN.

IF THE WORLD SEEMS COLD TO YOU, KINDLE FIRES TO WARM IT

www.ingramcontent.com/pod-product-compliance
Lightning Source LLC
Chambersburg PA
CBHW030900120726
48008CB00002B/56

* 9 7 9 8 8 9 4 7 5 9 1 3 5 *